PLANETS

AND THEIR MOONS

JOHN FARNDON

BookLife

INTRODUCTION

Have you ever wondered what lies in space beyond the comfort of our planet? There is a whole family of planets in the Solar System, many with their own moons.

This book will take you off into space, to explore Mercury and Venus, stopping at Earth and our Moon, and then on to Mars, Jupiter, Saturn, Uranus, Neptune and Pluto. Discover the amazing moons that orbit these planets and learn about other features found in the Solar System such as asteroids, comets and meteoroids.

SPOT
&
COUNT!

WATCH OUT FOR THESE CIRCLES TO LEARN MORE ABOUT THE TRULY WEIRD AND WONDERFUL FACTS ABOUT SPACE AND THE UNIVERSE IN WHICH WE LIVE. ★

FACT FOCUS

SPACE BITS

Look out for these boxes to take a closer look at space features.

ZOOM

Q: Why watch out for these boxes?

★ ★ ★

A: They give answers to the space questions you always wanted to ask.

Q&A

THIS EDITION:
2016 © BOOK LIFE
KING'S LYNN
PE30 4HG
FIRST PUBLISHED:
©ALADDIN BOOKS LTD
PO BOX 53987
LONDON SW15 2SF

ISBN: 978-1-910512-18-0

A CATALOGUE RECORD FOR THIS BOOK IS AVAILABLE FROM THE BRITISH LIBRARY.

PRINTED: MALAYSIA

ALL RIGHTS RESERVED

DESIGNED BY:
IAN McMULLEN

EDITED BY:
GRACE JONES

THE SOLAR SYSTEM

The Earth doesn't just hang in space. It zooms at the amazing speed of almost 107,000 km/h around the Sun. Earth isn't alone. Another eight huge balls, called planets, circle around the Sun too – all held in place by the pull of the Sun's gravity. The Sun and all its circling companions are together, called the Solar System.

HOW MANY PLANETS ARE IN THE SOLAR SYSTEM?

JUPITER

URANUS

FACT FOCUS

THE SOLAR SYSTEM IS AT LEAST 20 BILLION KM ACROSS. IF EARTH WERE THE SIZE OF A GRAIN OF SALT, THE SOLAR SYSTEM WOULD BE ABOUT AS BIG AS AN OLYMPIC STADIUM.

★

PLUTO

NEPTUNE

SATURN

Scientists have worked out that the Solar System was formed 4,560 million years ago. At first, it was just a dark whirling mass of gas and dust. But as it spun, gravity pulled bits tighter together. The dense centre became the Sun, and dust further out came together to form the planets.

Originally Pluto – discovered in 1930 – was classified as the ninth planet in the Solar System. In 2006 it was reclassified as a 'dwarf planet' – a planet that has a lower mass than others within its orbit. There are now only eight recognised planets in the Solar System.

The four planets closest to the Sun are Mercury, Venus, Earth and Mars. They are all quite small and are made mainly of rock. The next four planets are Jupiter, Saturn, Uranus and Neptune. They are all gas giants and are made of hydrogen, helium and other gases. The furthest planet, Pluto, is very small and made of rock.

THERE ARE 68 MOONS IN THE SOLAR SYSTEM.

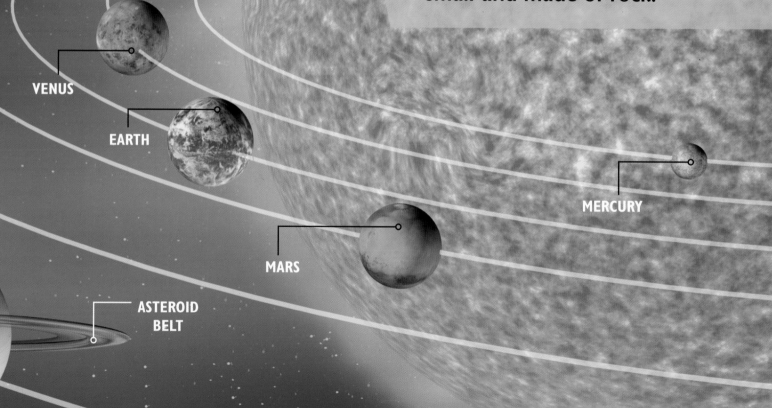

SUN

VENUS

EARTH

MERCURY

MARS

ASTEROID BELT

MERCURY

Mercury is the nearest planet to the Sun, less than 58 million km away. Mercury has little atmosphere to protect it, so the side facing the Sun is scorched (up to 430°C), while the dark side is icy cold (-180°C).

Q: If Mercury takes 59 days to turn round, how come the Sun stays up for 176 days?

★ ★ ★

A: Mercury rotates slowly, but whizzes round the Sun in just 88 days (compared to 365 days for the Earth). This means that as it turns slowly away from the Sun, it whizzes round the other side so that the sunny side is still facing the Sun.

MERCURY'S SURFACE

Mercury is small, so its gravity is weak and can't hold onto an atmosphere. There is nothing to protect the planet from the Sun's rays or stop meteors bashing into it. So it is even more deeply dented with craters than the Moon. A journey across the surface would show you nothing more than vast, empty basins, cliffs hundreds of kilometres long and yellow dust everywhere.

Mercury is smaller than some of Jupiter's moons. It is 20 times lighter than the Earth and barely a third of the diameter.

MERCURY

MERCURY'S CRATERS ARE NAMED AFTER SHAKESPEARE, BACH AND OTHER FAMOUS WRITERS AND COMPOSERS.

MERCURY

EVERY SO OFTEN, MERCURY PASSES ACROSS THE FACE OF THE SUN WHEN SEEN FROM THE EARTH.

FACT FOCUS

LIKE EARTH, MERCURY HAS POLAR ICE CAPS – BUT THE ICE IS MADE FROM ACID!
★

EARTH TURNS ROUND ONCE ON ITS AXIS IN 23 HOURS 56 MINUTES. MERCURY TAKES NEARLY 59 EARTH DAYS TO TURN ONCE ROUND ITS AXIS.

VENUS

Venus is almost exactly the same size as the Earth. It measures about 12,000 km across and weighs just a little less than the Earth. It is sometimes called the Evening Star or the Morning Star. This is because it is quite close to the Sun, so it can be seen in the night sky just after sunset and just before sunrise.

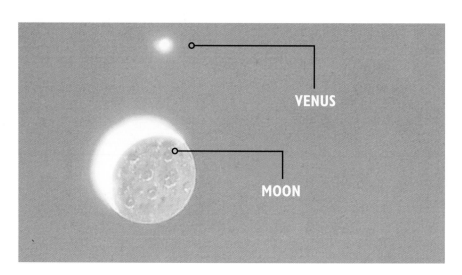

VENUS

MOON

When our Moon is a new crescent moon, it is between the Earth and the Sun. Venus lies between the Earth and the Sun too. So sometimes you will see Venus near the new Moon as it rises.

ZOOM

ATMOSPHERE

Venus is a beautiful planet covered in swirls of pinky white cloud. But the pink clouds are actually made partly of sulphuric acid. They are so thick that they press down on the planet's surface hard enough to crush a car!

COMPUTER RECONSTRUCTION
OF VENUS'S SURFACE

FACT FOCUS

HUGE AMOUNTS
OF CARBON DIOXIDE IN
VENUS'S ATMOSPHERE TRAP
HEAT ON THE SURFACE AND
BOOST TEMPERATURES TO
A SCORCHING 470°C, THE
HOTTEST IN THE SOLAR
SYSTEM.
★

The surface
of Venus can't be seen
since it is hidden
behind swirls of pinky
white cloud. It was
probably once covered
in huge oceans, but
they all boiled away. All
that is left are just hot,
bone-dry, rolling plains
dotted with volcanoes
and vast plateaus, such
as Lakshmi Plateau.

PLANET EARTH

Earth is the third planet out from the Sun, about 150 million km away. It is not so close to the Sun that it is scorching hot, nor so far away that it is icy cold. It has water on its surface, and can sustain life.

Q&A

Q: Why can we live on our planet?

★ ★ ★

A: Earth is a special place. It is the only planet we know that has water on its surface, and water makes life possible. It also has a blanket of gases, called the atmosphere, which we breathe.

THE EARTH IS MADE MOSTLY OF ROCK AND IS THE DENSEST PLANET IN THE SOLAR SYSTEM. BUT IT IS NOT JUST A SOLID BALL. IT HAS A SHELL OR CRUST OF HARD ROCK.

BENEATH THAT IS A LAYER ALMOST 3,000 KM DEEP OF WARM PARTLY MELTED ROCK, CALLED THE MANTLE.

THE CENTRE IS A CORE MADE ENTIRELY OF HOT METAL, MOSTLY IRON.

70% OF THE EARTH IS OCEAN. CAN YOU SPOT THE LAND?

The Earth whizzes once around the Sun every year. It is slightly tilted over. So as it travels around the Sun, the zone on Earth nearest the Sun gradually shifts. This is what creates seasons – the part of the world nearest the Sun has summer, the part which is farthest away has winter. The equator has no seasons.

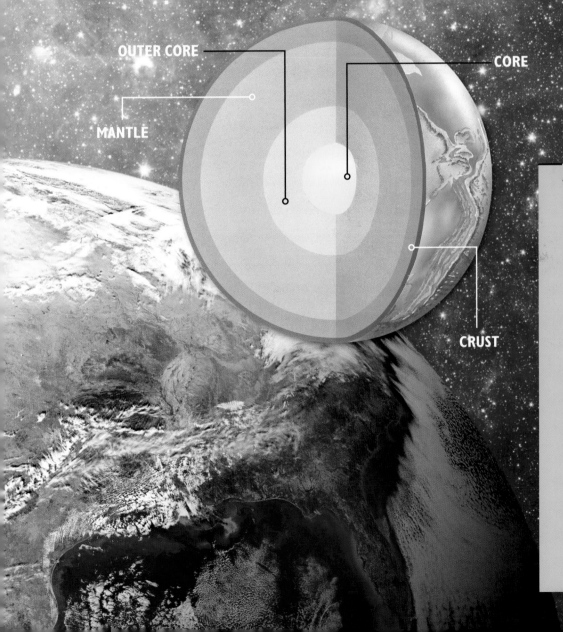

OUTER CORE

CORE

MANTLE

CRUST

ZOOM

EARTH IS NOT ROUND

The Earth is not quite round. The way the Earth spins makes it bulge out at the middle, round the equator. The Earth is 43 km narrower between the poles than around the equator.

OUR MOON

The Moon is Earth's companion. It is 384,400 km away, but that is very, very close in space terms. In fact, the Moon circles around the Earth about once a month – which is how we got the word 'month' (or 'moonth').

A SANDCASTLE BUILT ON THE MOON WOULD LAST FOREVER AS THERE IS NO WIND.

THE MOON IS A BARREN LIFELESS PLACE COVERED WITH DUST AND CRATERS CAUSED BY HUGE LUMPS OF ROCK CRASHING INTO IT BILLIONS OF YEARS AGO, WHEN THE MOON WAS YOUNG.

FACT FOCUS

THERE ARE HUGE DARK PATCHES ON THE MOON CALLED SEAS WHICH HAVE NEVER HAD A DROP OF WATER. THEY ARE PLAINS FORMED LONG AGO BY HOT MOLTEN ROCK FROM THE MOON'S INSIDE.

The Moon seems to change shape over a month. We only see the side of the Moon that is lit by the Sun. As the Moon circles the Earth, we see it from different angles – and so see more or less of its sunlit side.

At the new moon (1), we see a thin crescent shaped sliver. This grows over the next two weeks to a full moon (3), when we see all the sunlit side. It then shrinks back over the rest of the month to a crescent-shape – the old moon (5).

A LARGE OBJECT HITS THE EARTH. THE OBJECT MELTS AND SPLASHES OF DEBRIS FLY INTO SPACE.

DEBRIS SPINS IN ORBIT AND JOINS TOGETHER TO FORM THE MOON.

Q: How was the Moon made?

A: Amazingly, the Moon was probably made by a space collision. About 4,500 million years ago, soon after the Earth formed, a planet at least as big as Mars collided with Earth. The crash completely melted the other planet and splashes flew off into space. Gradually, gravity pulled these splashes together into a ball which cooled to form the Moon.

MARS

THE MAN WHO DISCOVERED MARS'S MOONS NAMED THEM PHOBOS... 'FEAR' AND DEIMOS... 'PANIC!'

Mars is the only planet to have an atmosphere or daytime temperatures anything like ours. But Mars is a desert planet, with no oceans or any sign of life – just red rocks and dust and a pink sky.

Q: Are there any volcanoes on Mars?

★ ★ ★

A: Like Earth and Venus, Mars has volcanoes. In fact, Olympus Mons (below) on Mars is the biggest volcano in the Solar System – three times higher than Mount Everest!

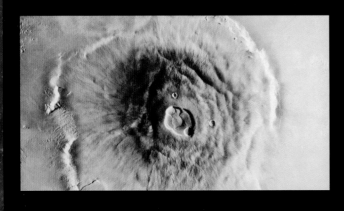

ZOOM

WATER ON MARS

In the 1880s, astronomers thought dark lines they saw on Mars's surface were actually canals built by Martians. They proved to be optical illusions, but valleys show water once flowed over the surface in abundance.

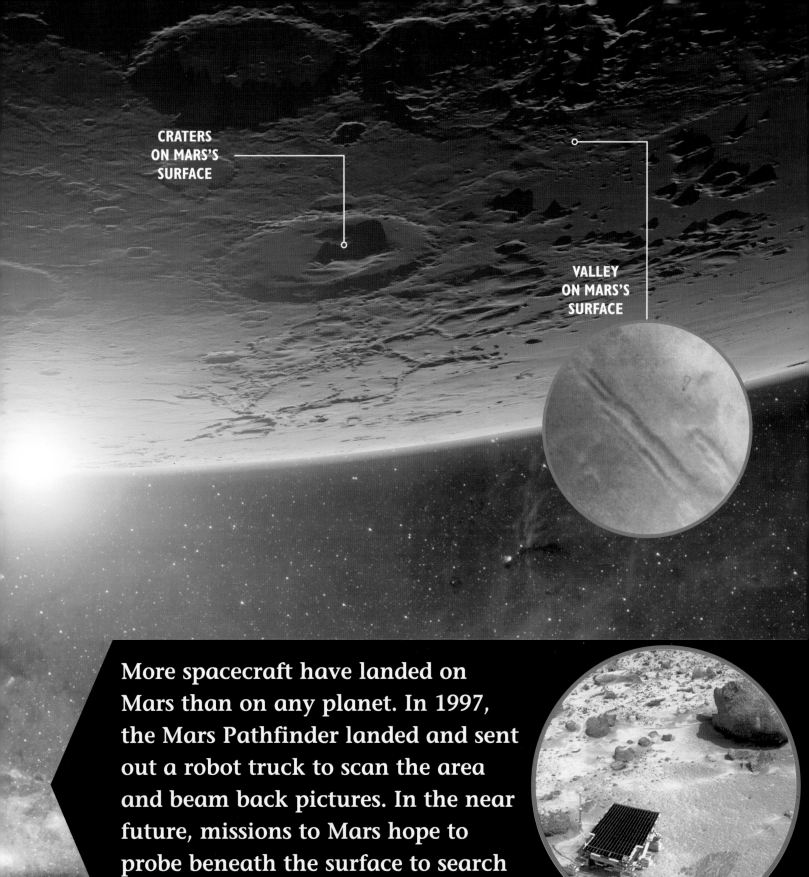

CRATERS
ON MARS'S
SURFACE

VALLEY
ON MARS'S
SURFACE

More spacecraft have landed on Mars than on any planet. In 1997, the Mars Pathfinder landed and sent out a robot truck to scan the area and beam back pictures. In the near future, missions to Mars hope to probe beneath the surface to search for signs of microscopic life.

ASTEROIDS, COMETS

There are hundreds of thousands of tiny pieces of rock and ice whizzing round the Sun, including asteroids, comets and meteoroids. Some are no bigger than sultanas, but the biggest asteroid, Ceres, is 933 km across. Two asteroids even have their own moons.

A meteoroid is dirt and debris from an asteroid or comet. It can be seen as a meteor as it burns in Earth's atmosphere. If it reaches Earth, usually no bigger than a lump of coal, it is called a meteorite. Comets are like huge dirty snowballs in the outer reaches of the Solar System. A comet's core is just a few kilometres across, but when it swings in close to the Sun and partly melts, it throws out a vast glistening tail of dust and gas.

ASTEROID

COMET

METEORITE

& METEOROIDS

THE METEOR CRATER IN ARIZONA IS A VAST BOWL THAT FORMED WHEN A METEORITE CRASHED INTO THE ARIZONA DESERT 50,000 YEARS AGO. THE IMPACT CREATED A HOLE OVER 1,200 M ACROSS AND 200 M DEEP.

THE CRATERS ON ASTEROID GASPRA ARE NAMED AFTER BEACHES.

Q&A

Q: Where are most asteroids found?

★ ★ ★

A: Most asteroids circle the Sun in a huge band between Mars and Jupiter called the asteroid belt. It may be the last remnants of a smashed planet. There are 26 asteroids that are over 200 km across, over a million that are at least 1 km across and billions of smaller bits!

HALLEY'S COMET IS VISIBLE FOR SEVERAL

JUPITER

Jupiter is gigantic. It is by far the biggest planet in the Solar System – over 140,000 km across – and it takes 12 years to go around the Sun. It is a huge ball of gas, more like the Sun than the Earth, and is made mostly of hydrogen and helium. You can see it clearly for part of the year. It is brighter than any of the stars.

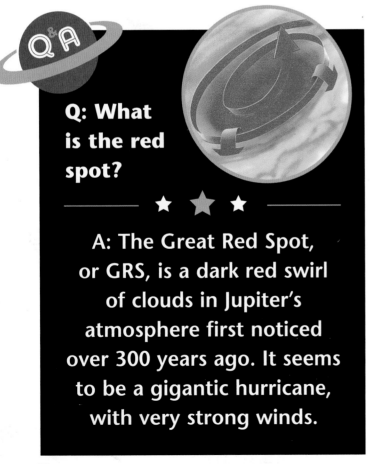

Q&A

Q: What is the red spot?

⭐ ⭐ ⭐

A: The Great Red Spot, or GRS, is a dark red swirl of clouds in Jupiter's atmosphere first noticed over 300 years ago. It seems to be a gigantic hurricane, with very strong winds.

Jupiter weighs 318 times as much as the Earth. Its colourful clouds are whipped into long belts by violent winds, which blow at up to 500 km/h.

JUPITER TURNS RIGHT ROUND IN UNDER 10 HOURS, COMPARED TO 24 HOURS FOR EARTH. AT JUPITER'S EQUATOR, THE SURFACE IS WHIZZING ROUND AT OVER 47,000 KM/H!

★

Jupiter's gravity is so powerful that it squeezes hydrogen and helium gases until they become liquid or solid. Under the thin atmosphere is an ocean of liquid hydrogen and a small rocky core.

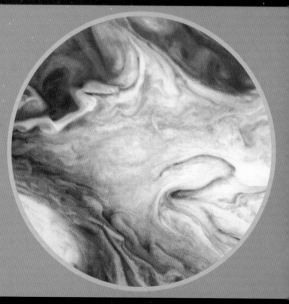

FIND THE GREAT RED SPOT.

JUPITER'S MOONS

Jupiter has at least 16 moons. The four largest (Io, Europa, Ganymede and Callisto) were discovered by a scientist called Galileo in 1610. Ganymede and Callisto are larger than our own Moon, and the other two are not much smaller.

ZOOM

EUROPA'S OCEANS

Europa has a very bright, smooth surface of ice with liquid water beneath. Scientists think that there might be life forms in this water. In places, the surface of Europa is cracked like an egg shell.

FACT FOCUS

JUPITER HAS 16 KNOWN MOONS BUT THERE MAY BE OTHERS TOO SMALL TO HAVE BEEN SEEN YET. YOU CAN SEE THE FOUR BIGGEST MOONS WITH AN ORDINARY PAIR OF BINOCULARS!

IF YOU WERE ON GANYMEDE YOU WOULD SEE JUPITER IN THE SKY.

Io has been called the most volcanic body in the Solar System. When the Voyager 2 space probe passed it in 1979, it discovered that plumes of material were being shot out from Io's surface up to a height of 300 km. It was the first evidence of active volcanoes anywhere other than the Earth.

UNTIL GALILEO SAW THROUGH HIS TELESCOPE THAT JUPITER'S MOONS CIRCLED ROUND IT, PEOPLE THOUGHT THAT EVERYTHING IN THE UNIVERSE CIRCLED ROUND THE EARTH.

★

CALLISTO'S VALHALLA CRATER IS SO DARK... ...IT MAKES THE MOON LOOK LIKE A GIANT EYEBALL!

GALILEO

GANYMEDE

EUROPA

IO

CALLISTO

21

SATURN

SATURN IS SO LIGHT THAT IT WOULD FLOAT IN A GIANT BATH OF WATER.

Saturn is the second largest planet in the Solar System, it is over 120,000 km across. Around it circle not only an amazing halo of rings stretching out 70,000 km, but also, beyond the rings, at least 22 moons – more than any other planet.

Q: What are Saturn's rings made of?

★ ★ ★

A: Saturn's rings are bands of countless billions of tiny blocks of ice and dust, circling the planet endlessly. Each ring is thousands of kilometres wide.

1995 **2005** **2011**

2000 **2009**

CHANGING RINGS

We can see Saturn's rings more clearly if we look at it at certain angles at different times. In 1995, the rings were edge on and hard to see. In 2005, the rings were at a greater angle, giving us a clearer view.

FACT FOCUS

THE TEMPERATURE OF SATURN'S ROCKY CORE IS ABOUT TWICE AS HOT AS THE SURFACE TEMPERATURE OF THE SUN.

URANUS

Uranus is so far from the Sun that temperatures on its surface drop to -210°C. In this amazing cold, the methane (natural gas) that covers the planet turns to liquid oceans thousands of kilometres deep. It is these icy oceans that give Uranus its beautiful blue colour.

FACT FOCUS

BECAUSE URANUS ROLLS ROUND THE SUN ON ITS SIDE, THE SUN DOES SOME ODD THINGS. IN SPRING, THE SUN RISES AND SETS EVERY NINE HOURS – BACKWARDS!

Uranus tilts so far over that it's on its side. It spins round once every 17 hours, but this has no effect on the length of a day. Instead, the day depends on where Uranus is in its orbit. When the south pole is pointing directly at the Sun, the Sun doesn't go down there for 20 years!

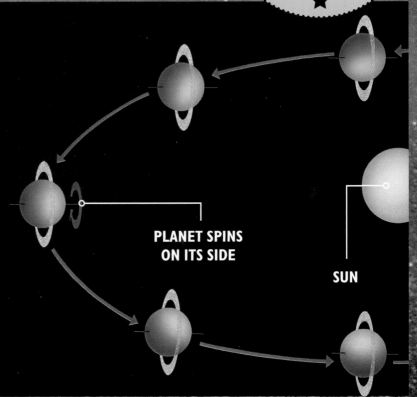

PLANET SPINS ON ITS SIDE

SUN

Uranus's icy atmosphere is made of hydrogen and helium. Winds whistle through it at over 2,000 km/h, ten times faster than the fastest hurricane on Earth. If you fell into its icy oceans for even a fraction of a second, you'd freeze so hard you could be shattered like glass.

ZOOM

LONG YEAR

Uranus is almost three billion kilometres from the Sun. This far out, the distance Uranus has to travel round the Sun is vast and takes over 84 Earth years.

URANUS'S MOON, OBERON

NEPTUNE

TRITON LOOKS LIKE A MELON WITH PINK ICE CREAM ON THE END!

Neptune is the fourth largest planet in the Solar System. It's so far from the Sun – about 4.5 billion km – that it takes 164.79 years to go around the Sun. Indeed, it hasn't even gone right around once since it was first discovered back in 1846.

Neptune is an icy blue planet like Uranus, covered in oceans of liquid methane. Surface temperatures on Neptune plunge to -210°C, – but its moon Triton is even colder, with temperatures a chilling 236°C below zero. Triton's surface is covered in volcanoes that erupt ice!

TRITON

SURFACE OF TRITON

CAN YOU SPOT THE CLOUDS ON NEPTUNE'S SURFACE?

GREAT DARK SPOTS APPEAR ON DIFFERENT PLACES ON NETUNE'S SURFACE.

CLOUD FEATURES ON NEPTUNE'S SURFACE.

ZOOM

SCOOTER

Neptune has raging storms and clouds on its surface that come and go over the years, probably driven by Neptune's internal heat. It also has a small white cloud of methane ice crystals that zips round the planet once every 16 hours and so is now known as the Scooter.

FACT FOCUS

NEPTUNE IS THE WINDIEST PLACE IN THE SOLAR SYSTEM, WITH WINDS OF OVER 2,500 KM/H! YOU COULD THROW A PAPER DART FASTER THAN THE FASTEST JET PLANE ON EARTH.

★

PLUTO

THE MOON ON PLUTO LOOKS 3 TIMES AS BIG AS OURS AND NEVER MOVES

Pluto is the most remote planet in the Solar System – a tiny, lonely world smaller than our Moon. It is so far from the Sun that the sun looks little bigger than a star in the sky and shines no brighter than the Moon. Sunlight only takes 8 minutes to reach Earth, but takes up to 6 hours to reach Pluto.

Q&A

Q: How big is Pluto compared to Earth?

★ ★ ★

A: Pluto is only 2274km across barely a fifth the size of Earth, and 500 times lighter. This is why Pluto was only discovered in 1930 – and is still very hard for astronomers to spot.

ZOOM

CHARLENE!

Charon was only discovered in 1978. The man who spotted it, American astronomer Jim Christy, was going to call it after his wife Charlene. But then he looked in a book of Greek myths and found Charon was the ferryman who took lost souls to the underworld, land of Pluto. So he called it Charon.

Pluto has an odd oval orbit. Most of the time, it is billions of kilometres out beyond Neptune. But for a year or two every three centuries, it actually moves in closer to the Sun than Neptune.

PLUTO'S ORBIT

NEPTUNE'S ORBIT

CHARON

PLUTO

Pluto has a moon almost half its size, called Charon. Pluto and Charon circle round each other. So Charon always stays in the same place in Pluto's sky, looking three times as big as our Moon.

Originally Pluto – discovered in 1930 – was classified as the ninth planet in the Solar System. In 2006 it was reclassified as a 'dwarf planet' – a planet that has a lower mass than others within its orbit. There are now only eight recognised planets in the Solar System.

PLANET FACTS

Use the table below to help you compare some fascinating facts about the nine planets in our Solar System.

PLANET	NO. OF MOONS	MASS X EARTH	DISTANCE FROM SUN (MILLIONS OF KILOMETERS)	LENGTH OF YEAR
MERCURY	0	0.055	58	88 DAYS
VENUS	0	0.82	108	225 DAYS
EARTH	1	1.00	150	365.5 DAYS
MARS	2	0.11	228	687 DAYS
JUPITER	16	317.8	778	11.9 DAYS
SATURN	22	95.2	1,432	29.5 DAYS
URANUS	15	14.5	2,871	84.1 DAYS
NEPTUNE	8	17.2	4,498	164.9 DAYS
PLUTO	1	0.002	5,914	248 DAYS

GLOSSARY

ASTEROIDS

SMALL, ROCKY OBJECTS, THE GREATEST COLLECTION OF WHICH ORBIT THE SUN IN A BAND CALLED THE ASTEROID BELT, BETWEEN MARS AND JUPITER.

ATMOSPHERE

THE LAYER OF GASES THAT SURROUND A PLANET. THE ATMOSPHERE AROUND THE EARTH SUPPLIES US WITH THE OXYGEN THAT KEEPS US ALIVE.

COMETS

LUMPS OF ICE AND DUST THAT ORBIT THE SUN. AS A COMET APPROACHES THE SUN, HEAT FROM THE SUN CAUSES THE ICE AND DUST TO BOIL OFF, CREATING HUGE TAILS THAT STRETCH OUT BEHIND THE COMET.

CRATER

A BOWL-SHAPED PIT ON THE SURFACE OF A PLANET. SOME ARE CAUSED BY VOLCANOES, AND SOME BY THE IMPACT OF A METEORITE.

EQUATOR

AN IMAGINARY LINE THAT RUNS AROUND THE MIDDLE OF A PLANET AT AN EQUAL DISTANCE FROM ITS TWO POLES.

GRAVITY

EVERY OBJECT IN THE UNIVERSE HAS A FORCE THAT ATTRACTS IT TO EVERY OTHER OBJECT. THIS FORCE IS CALLED GRAVITY. THE SOLAR SYSTEM IS HELD TOGETHER BY THE SUN'S GRAVITATIONAL PULL.

GREAT RED SPOT

A DARK RED SWIRL OF CLOUDS IN JUPITER'S ATMOSPHERE.

METEORITE

A METEOR THAT HITS THE EARTH'S SURFACE.

METEOROIDS

SMALL PIECES OF SPACE DEBRIS WHICH ORBIT THE SUN.

METEORS

OBJECTS THAT HIT THE EARTH'S ATMOSPHERE AND BURN UP LEAVING A FIERY TAIL THAT DISAPPEARS AFTER A FEW SECONDS.

MOONS

SMALL BODIES THAT ORBIT AROUND SOME OF THE MAJOR PLANETS. EARTH HAS ONE MOON, WHILE VENUS HAS NONE AND JUPITER HAS 16.

ORBIT

THE PATH OF AN OBJECT, SUCH AS A PLANET OR A COMET, AROUND ANOTHER OBJECT, SUCH AS A STAR.

PLANETS

LARGE OBJECTS THAT ORBIT AROUND A STAR. THESE CAN BE ROCKY PLANETS SUCH AS THE EARTH, VENUS OR MARS, OR GASSY GIANT PLANETS, SUCH AS JUPITER, SATURN OR URANUS.

POLE

A POINT ON A PLANET'S SURFACE AROUND WHICH THE PLANET SPINS OR ROTATES.

SOLAR SYSTEM

THE GROUP OF MAJOR PLANETS, INCLUDING EARTH, AND MINOR PLANETS THAT ORBIT THE SUN.

INDEX